KT-134-373

casseroles

tessa bramley

PHOTOGRAPHY BY CRAIG ROBERTSON

casseroles

COMFORT FOOD AT ITS BEST

RYLAND
PETERS
& SMALL

LONDON NEW YORK

Senior Designer   Paul Tilby
Editor   Maddalena Bastianelli
Production   Meryl Silbert
Art Director   Gabriella Le Grazie
Publishing Director Alison Starling

Food Stylist   Tessa Bramley
Stylist   Helen Trent

AUTHOR ACKNOWLEDGEMENTS

This book would not have been possible without the commitment and hard work of my staff at the Old Vicarage. My thanks, in particular, to Nathan and Andrew for backing me in all I do and for testing the recipes. Their good humour and technical skills have been invaluable – as always! Thanks also to Andrew and Carole (my son and daughter-in-law), for their inspiration and for selflessly eating their way through every dish. Many thanks to Mum, Howard and Linda for their support and continuous belief in me. Finally, I am indebted to my agent Fiona at Limelight and to the team at Ryland Peters & Small; especially Maddie for her endless patience with words, Paul for his beautiful design and Craig for his stunning photography. Thank you guys!

First published in Great Britain in 2000
by Ryland Peters & Small, Cavendish House,
51–55 Mortimer Street, London W1N 7TD

Text © Tessa Bramley 2000
Design and photographs © Ryland Peters & Small 2000

10 9 8 7 6 5 4 3 2 1

Printed and bound in China by Toppan Printing Co.

The author's moral rights have been asserted. All rights reserved. No part of this publication may be reproduced, stored in a retrieval system, or transmitted in any form or by any means, electronic, mechanical, photocopying or otherwise, without the prior permission of the publisher.

ISBN 1 84172 076 3

A CIP record for this book is available from the British Library.

Notes

All spoon measurements are level unless otherwise stated.

All fruits and vegetables should be washed thoroughly and peeled, unless otherwise stated. Unwaxed citrus fruits should be used whenever possible.

Specialist Asian ingredients are available in large supermarkets, Thai and Chinese shops, as well as Asian stores.

CONTENTS

A brief sauté followed by relaxed, gentle cooking in a moderate oven will melt tough meat fibres into tender sweetness. Casseroles, braises and pot-roasts are the convenience meals of today. They can be assembled quickly and ahead of time, are often marinated with herbs and aromatics for extra flavour, then left to cook undisturbed. This is delicious, comforting home-cooked food at its best.

INTRODUCTION

As a child, I remember my grandmother cooking wonderful slow-cooked meals. Her pot-roasts and casseroles would fill the whole house with delicious meaty aromas. Real home-cooking, using the best local home-grown ingredients and produce, is what I grew up on.

Casseroling is a simple, foolproof cooking technique. In fact, it's almost impossible for you to go wrong. First of all choose an ovenproof casserole dish with a tight-fitting lid. The size of the dish will depend on what you are cooking and for how many people, but in general, do not fill the casserole more than two-thirds full. A flameproof casserole is better still. As most recipes require you to brown vegetables or sear meat in hot oil or butter first (to add colour and flavour), you can save time – and washing up – if this can be done in the same cookware that will transfer to the oven. However, a heavy-based frying pan is just as good for browning and searing. It is useful – and fun – to have a selection of casserole dishes to fit the contents as well as the occasion.

Homemade stock will always give your casserole the best flavour. Try to get into the habit of making your own, then you can refrigerate or freeze it until needed. Put the carcass of birds, meat or fish bones in a large stockpot or saucepan, add vegetables, such as carrots, onions and celery and fill with cold water. Throw in some fresh herbs, if using, and freshly cracked black pepper. Boil, then simmer. Skim off the scum. For chicken and meat stocks, simmer for 1 hour, but simmer fish stock for 20 minutes only or it will become bitter. Strain before using. Supermarkets now sell tubs of fresh stock, so you could use this if you don't have time to make your own. Use the appropriate stock for the kind of meat you are cooking: chicken for chicken casseroles, beef for beef dishes, and so on. Wine adds flavour too. In general, use a full-bodied red wine for dark meat and a robust, dry white wine for white meat and fish.

Flavours develop, concentrate and meld together in a moist-cooking medium when ingredients are casseroled, pot-roasted or braised. Long, slow-cooking tenderizes meat, so less expensive, tougher cuts can be used. The connective tissue in the meat melts into the cooking liquid to give a thick, juicy sauce. To finish, creamy mashed potatoes, fluffy rice or crusty country-style bread are all you need to complete a hearty meal.

OVEN-BAKED CHOWDER

This chunky fish and vegetable stew often includes salt pork and potatoes. Some recipes call for tomatoes or sweetcorn as well. In Brittany, soups are cooked in a pot called a *chaudière*, and maybe the name chowder was derived from this. Chowders are a speciality of New England, where they are often made with shellfish, particularly clams. I like to make mine with Venus clams, which are much sweeter and more tender than the larger varieties. This one-pot meal is easy to make and perfect for a warming supper.

Put the salt pork or bacon in a large, deep frying pan and fry until crisp and golden. Remove to a plate. Add the onion and celeriac to the bacon fat in the pan and cook until browned. Remove to a plate.

Blanch the potatoes in salted boiling water for 1 minute, then drain. Heat the butter in the frying pan, add the flour and cook, stirring for 1 minute. Gradually add the hot milk, beating until the sauce is smooth and thickened. Add the fried vegetables, potatoes and 500 ml water. Mix well, then pour into a casserole. Stir in the corn.

Cover and cook in a preheated oven at 170°C (325°F) Gas 3 for about 1 hour until the vegetables are soft and start to fall apart. Remove from the oven, add the cod or haddock and cover: the heat of the stew will cook the fish.

Meanwhile, put the clams or mussels in a roasting tin and put in the oven for 2–3 minutes until the shells open. Discard any that have not opened. Remove the shellfish and strain any juices left in the shells. Add the shellfish, juices, cream and nutmeg to the chowder and stir gently to mix. Heat through and add salt and pepper to taste. Ladle into 4 deep dishes and serve with chopped chives or parsley.

200 g rindless salt pork or streaky bacon, diced

2 onions, finely chopped

1 celeriac, about 500 g, finely chopped

25 g unsalted butter

1 tablespoon flour

500 ml hot milk

350 g potatoes, diced

100 g fresh corn kernels

500 g cod or haddock fillet, skinned, boned and cut into large chunks

1 kg clams or mussels, cleaned

150 ml double cream

1/4 teaspoon freshly grated nutmeg

sea salt and freshly ground black pepper

chopped fresh chives or parsley, to serve

SERVES 4

FISH and SHELLFISH

This traditional Scottish stew - known as *Cullen Skink* - is made with smoked Finnan haddock, thickened with potatoes and enriched with a splash of cream. If you can't get this fish, use another naturally smoked haddock instead. Don't be tempted to use the vibrant yellow variety, as this is artificially coloured and does not have such a good flavour.

SMOKED HADDOCK STEW
with potatoes and celeriac

Heat the butter in a large saucepan, add the onions, potatoes and celeriac and cook, stirring until softened. Add the fish stock, 250 ml water and pepper. Bring to the boil, then pour into a casserole.

Cover and cook in a preheated oven at 150°C (300°F) Gas 2 for 50 minutes or until the potatoes and celeriac have disintegrated into the liquid and the mixture has thickened. Remove from the oven.

Pour the milk into the casserole. Put the smoked haddock, skin side up, on top of the vegetables and return to the oven for a further 4–5 minutes until the fish is cooked. Remove from the oven and take out the haddock. Peel off and discard the skin and bones. Flake the fish with a fork and set aside.

Stir the cream into the casserole and reheat. Return the fish to the casserole, then serve in deep dishes with the chopped parsley.

VARIATION:

For a smoother soup-stew, after removing the fish from the casserole, press the remaining mixture through a coarse sieve. Proceed with the recipe and add extra milk or cream, if necessary.

25 g unsalted butter

2 onions, finely chopped

250 g potatoes, diced

1 celeriac, about 500 g, finely chopped

250 ml fish stock

500 ml hot milk

1 kg undyed smoked haddock, preferably Finnan

about 150 ml double cream

a large handful of fresh parsley, chopped, to serve

sea salt and freshly ground black pepper

SERVES 4

Turbot is a meaty fish that's ideal for casseroling, with the juices in the pot keeping it moist. Rubbed with this wonderful spice mix, the fish can be left for up to 2 hours for the flavours to intensify. I like to rub thickly sliced French bread with garlic and olive oil, pop it in on a tray and put it in the oven to crisp. It's delicious with the fish.

CUMIN and CORIANDER SPICED TURBOT
with chillies

Heat 2 tablespoons of the oil in a frying pan, add the leeks and celeriac and cook until just golden. Transfer to a casserole and season with salt and pepper. Dry-roast the spice seeds in a non-stick frying pan for 2 minutes to release the aromas. Let cool, lightly crush with a pestle and mortar, then rub half onto the turbot and refrigerate until needed.

Heat 2 tablespoons of the oil in the frying pan, add the shallots or onions, chillies and garlic and fry until just softened. Add the remaining spice mix and mix well. Add the saffron and a few tablespoons of the wine. Cook briefly until the colour and flavour emerge from the saffron. Season lightly. Pour in the remaining wine, bring to the boil and add to the casserole. Cover and cook in a preheated oven at 170°C (325°F) Gas 3 for 30 minutes until softened.

Heat the remaining oil in a non-stick frying pan and lightly brown the fish on one side. Put it on top of the vegetables in the casserole and surround it with the courgettes. Season lightly.

Return to the oven and cook uncovered for 10 minutes until the fish is cooked and the courgettes are bright green. Using a slotted spoon, transfer the fish and vegetables to a deep dish and keep them warm.

Strain the cooking liquid into a saucepan and bring to the boil. Add the cream and cook until reduced and thickened. Pour the sauce over the fish and vegetables and serve with the chopped coriander.

6 tablespoons olive oil

3 leeks, trimmed and thickly sliced

1 celeriac, about 500 g, cut into large chunks

4 teaspoons cumin seeds

4 teaspoons coriander seeds

black seeds from 18 green cardamom pods, crushed

6 shallots or 2 small onions, finely chopped

3 green chillies, deseeded and finely sliced

3 fat garlic cloves, finely sliced

1 large pinch of saffron threads

750 ml dry white wine

2 turbot fillets, about 500 g each, skinned, boned and cut in half

3 courgettes, sliced diagonally

250 ml double cream

a large handful of fresh coriander, chopped

salt and freshly ground mixed peppercorns

SERVES 4

Lift the small fillet on the underside of each chicken breast and insert a sage leaf. Season with salt and pepper and set aside. Peel and trim the vegetables, then cut into evenly-sized chunks, but leave the shallots whole. Set aside.

Heat the stock in a large saucepan until boiling. Add the chicken thighs and legs, reduce the heat and simmer for about 20 minutes. Drain, reserving the stock.

Put the chicken breasts, carrots and parsnips in a large, shallow ovenproof dish. Add 2–3 sprigs of the sage and the thyme. Season with salt and pepper. Add the part-cooked chicken thighs and legs and enough hot stock to cover. Cook, covered, in a preheated oven at 180°C (350°F) Gas 4 for about 45 minutes or until the juices run clear when a chicken thigh is pierced.

Remove from the oven. Using a slotted spoon, take out the chicken pieces and half the vegetables and keep them warm.

Put the remaining vegetables and cooking liquid in a food processor or blender and whiz to a purée. Strain into a large saucepan. Chop the remaining sage and add to the pan with the cream. Heat until the sauce has reduced and thickened slightly. Season to taste.

Return the chicken and vegetables to the dish, add the leeks and pour over the sauce. Cook for a further 20–25 minutes until the chicken is cooked and the vegetables are golden and glazed. Serve with sage leaves or flowers, if using, and buttered cabbage.

16 free-range, small chicken pieces, including breasts, thighs and legs

7–8 sprigs of sage

6 carrots

4 small thin leeks

4 parsnips

16 shallots

1.75 litres chicken stock

3–4 sprigs of thyme

150 ml double cream

salt and freshly ground black pepper

sage leaves or flowers, to serve (optional)

SERVES 4

CHICKEN, SAGE and PARSNIP CASSEROLE

With bold, gutsy flavours and a surprisingly silky sauce, this dish won't fail to impress. It's perfect for an elegant dinner party and is made even more stylish if scattered with sage flowers.

POULTRY and GAME

Lift the skin of the chicken pieces and tuck a few tarragon leaves between the skin and flesh. Season with salt and freshly ground black pepper.

Using a sharp knife, cut long strips of zest from the lemons (leaving the bitter white pith). Squeeze and reserve the juice. Blanch a strip of peel in boiling water, remove and plunge into iced water to cool. When cold, cut into fine shreds and reserve.

Heat half the butter in a heavy-based frying pan until foaming, then add the chicken pieces and brown on all sides. Transfer to a casserole and add the strips of lemon zest.

Heat the remaining butter in the same frying pan, add the onion and saffron threads and fry until the onion is softened. Add the lemon juice and sugar, if using, and bring to the boil. Add the stock and return to the boil. Stir in half the cream, salt and pepper, then add to the casserole. Cover with a lid.

To make the tarragon potatoes, put the potatoes on a sheet of foil, add the butter, tarragon and salt. Bring the edges of the foil together and scrunch to seal.

Cook the casserole and potatoes in a preheated oven at 180°C (350°F) Gas 4 for about 1-1½ hours, or until cooked. To test if the chicken is done, insert a knife into the thickest part of a chicken thigh and the juices should run clear. If not, cook for 10 minutes more, then test again. Remove the chicken and potatoes and keep them warm.

Pour the cooking liquid into a saucepan. Discard the lemon zest. Add the remaining cream and heat until reduced and caramelized. Add salt and pepper to taste.

Put the chicken on a serving plate, pour over the sauce and top with the reserved lemon shreds and remaining tarragon. Serve with the tarragon potatoes.

POT-ROASTED CHICKEN
with saffron and lemon

A light chicken casserole, combining the freshness of lemon with the heady scent and colour of saffron. Scatter with a handful of tarragon and serve with foil-baked buttery potatoes for a fresh spring treat.

16 free-range, small chicken pieces, including breasts, thighs and legs

a handful of fresh tarragon

2 small, thin-skinned unwaxed lemons

1 onion, finely chopped

2 large pinches of saffron threads

1 tablespoon caster sugar (optional)

500 ml chicken stock

50 g unsalted butter

250 ml double cream

sea salt and freshly ground black pepper

TARRAGON POTATOES:

500 g small new potatoes, scrubbed

50 g unsalted butter

a handful of fresh tarragon

sea salt

SERVES 4

In the north of England and Scotland, pearl barley is used to thicken and enrich soups, broths and stews; it was certainly one of my grandmother's favourites. The long, slow cooking of this broth means the chicken will be meltingly tender and will literally fall off the bone. Comforting and warming, it is perfect on a cold, windy night. Pheasant or rabbit can be used for a richer, darker broth.

CHICKEN BROTH with pearl barley and rosemary

25 g unsalted butter

16 free-range, small chicken pieces, including breasts, thighs and legs

1 onion, finely chopped

2 carrots, diced

2 leeks, diced

2 celery stalks, diced

250 ml red wine

2 fresh bay leaves

1 sprig of rosemary

8 juniper berries, crushed

50 g pearl barley

2 potatoes, diced

2 litres chicken stock

sea salt and freshly ground black pepper

TO SERVE: (optional)

chopped fresh parsley or chives

sour cream

SERVES 4

Heat half the butter in a large frying pan, add the chicken pieces and fry until browned on all sides. Remove and put in a deep casserole. Season lightly with salt and freshly ground black pepper.

Add the remaining butter to the pan, add the onion, carrots, leeks and celery and cook until softened and the butter has been absorbed. Transfer to the casserole.

Put the wine, bay leaves, rosemary, juniper berries, salt and pepper in a saucepan and bring to the boil. Pour into the casserole. Put the pearl barley, potatoes and stock into the pan, bring to the boil and add to the casserole.

Cover and cook in a preheated oven at 170°C (325°F) Gas 3 for about 1 hour, then reduce to 150°C (300°F) Gas 2 and cook, uncovered, for a further 1–1½ hours until thickened.

Remove and discard the bay leaves and rosemary and add salt and pepper to taste. To serve, ladle the broth into heated, deep soup plates, sprinkle with chopped parsley or chives and add a swirl of sour cream, if using.

We all have a favourite recipe for *coq au vin*, so I thought it would be interesting to use a gutsy white wine instead of the traditional red. The prunes add extra richness and flavour, but you can omit them if you want to. *Coq au vin rouge* it's not, but delicious nonetheless.

COQ AU VIN BLANC

4 tablespoons olive oil

100 g pancetta or bacon, diced

20 shallots, 4 finely chopped and 16 left whole

2 garlic cloves, finely chopped

50 g unsalted butter

250 g button mushrooms

8 free-range chicken quarters

2 tablespoons seasoned flour

2 fresh bay leaves

4–5 sprigs of thyme

4–5 sprigs of parsley

12 no-soak prunes, pitted

500 ml full-bodied, dry white wine

250 ml chicken stock

2 tablespoons Amontillado or other medium dry sherry

sea salt and freshly ground mixed peppercorns

SERVES 4

Heat 1 tablespoon of the oil in a deep frying pan, add the pancetta or bacon and fry until crisp. Remove with a slotted spoon and set aside. Add the chopped shallots and garlic to the bacon fat in the pan and fry until lightly golden. Remove and set aside.

Heat half the butter and 1 tablespoon of the oil in the same pan, add the whole shallots and mushrooms and fry until lightly golden. Remove and set aside.

Toss the chicken pieces in the seasoned flour until lightly coated. Heat the remaining oil in the same frying pan, add the chicken pieces and fry until golden (cook in batches, if necessary). Put the chicken and vegetables in a casserole. Tuck in the bay leaves and add the thyme, parsley and prunes. Season.

Heat the wine and stock in saucepan until just boiling, then pour it over the chicken and vegetables. Cover and cook in a preheated oven at 180°C (350°F) Gas 4 for about 1½ hours or until the chicken is done. To test, insert a skewer into the thickest part of a thigh and juices should run clear. If not, cook for 10 minutes more and test again.

Remove the chicken and vegetables and keep them hot. Strain the cooking liquid and reserve. Heat the sherry in a saucepan until reduced by half to burn off the alcohol and concentrate the flavour. Add the reserved liquid, return to the boil and cook until reduced by half.

Whisk in the remaining butter, in small pieces, to thicken the sauce and give it a glossy finish.

Serve the chicken and vegetables with the sauce poured over.

Using a sharp knife, make small incisions in the turkey rolls and insert the garlic slivers and coriander.

Melt the butter in a heavy-based frying pan until foaming, then add the turkey and sear until golden on all sides. Remove and put into a casserole.

Add the onion, chopped garlic and chillies to the same frying pan and cook until softened. Transfer to the casserole. Pour the wine into the pan, bring to the boil and cook until reduced by half. Add the stock and return to the boil.

Remove and discard the outer layer of the lemongrass, then crush the stems with a rolling pin or heavy knife to release the flavour. Add to the pan.

Add the coconut milk, return to the boil and season. Pour over the turkey and vegetables and cook, uncovered, in a preheated oven at 200°C (400°F) Gas 6 for about 20 minutes. Cover, reduce to 180°C (350°F) Gas 4 and cook for a further 1½ hours until tender. For the last 15 minutes of cooking, remove the lid and increase to 200°C (400°F) Gas 6 to brown the turkey.

Slice the turkey and serve with the sauce, Thai fragrant rice and coriander.

2 turkey thighs, boned, rolled and tied (ask your butcher to do this)

4 fat garlic cloves, 2 cut into slivers and 2 finely chopped

a handful of fresh coriander

25 g unsalted butter

1 onion, finely chopped

3 hot red chillies, deseeded and finely sliced into rings

250 ml white wine

250 ml turkey or chicken stock

2 stalks lemongrass

400 ml canned coconut milk

sea salt and freshly ground mixed peppercorns

TO SERVE:

Thai fragrant rice

a handful of fresh coriander

SERVES 4

Turkey thighs are relatively inexpensive. The dark meat has a richer flavour than the lighter breast meat – and it is a perfect match for the distinctive flavours of Thai cooking.

BRAISED TURKEY
with coconut and lemongrass

CASSEROLED DUCK with fresh figs

Fruity sweet figs counterbalance the rich duck. Look for deep purple-skinned ones and make sure they are fully ripe for the best flavour.

Remove the skin from the duck breasts. Heat a cast-iron frying pan, add the skins and fry until the fat runs. Discard the skins but reserve the fat. Meanwhile, lift the small fillet on the underside of each breast and insert a few sage leaves. Season all the duck pieces.

Add the onion, celery and chopped leeks to the duck fat in the pan and fry until lightly golden. Transfer to an ovenproof dish or roasting tin. Add the sherry to the pan and heat, stirring, until reduced to a sticky glaze. Pour in the wine, bring to the boil and cook until reduced by half. Add the stock, return to the boil and pour on top of the vegetables. Add the chopped figs, then top with the duck legs, skin side up.

Cook, uncovered, in a preheated oven at 190°C (375°F) Gas 5 for about 1–1½ hours, basting the duck from time to time with the pan juices.

Blanch the remaining leeks in boiling salted water for 1 minute to soften, then drain and add to the baking dish. Lay the duck breasts on top of the vegetables and baste with the juices. Cook, uncovered, for a further 10-12 minutes until the legs are well done and the skin is crispy and the breasts still slightly pink. Remove the duck and the pieces of leek and keep them hot.

To make the sauce, strain the cooking liquid into a saucepan, pressing the vegetables and figs through the sieve with the back of a wooden spoon to extract all the flavour. Cook over a high heat until slightly thickened. To finish, whisk in the butter, a little at a time, until the sauce is glossy and thick. Season to taste. Add the fig quarters and heat through.

Put the duck, leeks and figs into a deep serving plate, pour over the sauce and serve – fabulous!

8 pieces of lean, oven-ready duck, including breasts and legs

5–6 sprigs of sage

1 onion, chopped

2 celery stalks, chopped

3 leeks, 1 chopped and 2 cut into 2.5 cm pieces

4 tablespoons Amontillado or other medium dry sherry

250 ml full-bodied red wine

750 ml duck or chicken stock

8 fresh figs, 4 coarsely chopped and 4 quartered

25 g unsalted butter

sea salt and freshly ground black pepper

SERVES 4

Season the duck pieces with salt and pepper. Using a sharp knife, make 2-3 shallow, diagonal cuts in the duck breasts.

Heat a cast-iron frying pan and dry-fry the breasts, skin side down, until the fat runs and the skin is crisp and golden. Remove and set aside.

Add the onion, garlic, potatoes and celeriac to the duck fat in the pan and fry until golden. (Add a little of the butter, if necessary.) Transfer to the casserole. Put the duck thighs in the frying pan, fry until golden, then add to the casserole. Tuck in the sprigs of rosemary.

Pour the port into the frying pan and heat, stirring to deglaze the pan juices, and cook until reduced by half. Add the wine, return to the boil and reduce again by half. Pour it over the vegetables and duck thighs. Heat the stock until boiling, then add to the casserole. Cover and cook in a preheated oven at 170°C (325°F) Gas 3 for 1 hour.

Reserve 1 tablespoon of the blueberries, then put the rest in a small saucepan, add the sugar and cook until the fruit is soft and pulpy. Push through a sieve to remove the seeds and give a deep red purée.

Remove the casserole from the oven, add the part-cooked breasts, skin side up, and stir in the fruit purée. Increase to 200°C (400°F) Gas 6 and cook, uncovered, for 20-25 minutes until the duck thighs are meltingly tender and the breasts crisp but still slightly pink. Using a slotted spoon, remove the vegetables and duck pieces to a heated serving dish and keep them warm. Remove and discard the rosemary sprigs. Add the reserved blueberries.

Pour the cooking liquid into a saucepan, add salt and pepper and bring to the boil. If you prefer a thicker sauce, whisk in the butter - a little at a time - until glossy and slightly thickened. Pour the sauce over the duck and serve with buttered spinach.

4 lean, oven-ready duck breasts and 4 thighs

1 red onion, chopped

2 garlic cloves, finely chopped

3 medium potatoes, cut into chunks

1 celeriac, about 500 g, cut into chunks

25 g unsalted butter (optional)

2 sprigs of rosemary

150 ml ruby port

150 ml red wine

250 ml duck or chicken stock

150 g blueberries

1 tablespoon sugar

sea salt and freshly ground black pepper

SERVES 4

DUCK with blueberries and rosemary

You can make your own duck stock using duck bones and drumsticks. Blueberries complement the rich flavour of duck, but you can also use blackberries when in season.

The bacon jacket protects the guinea fowl, keeping it moist and succulent while cooking. Try to use free-range birds if you can as they have the best flavour. For a crispy bacon wrapping, cook in a shallow, ovenproof gratin dish.

GUINEA FOWL WRAPPED in BACON
with cinnamon and port

2 guinea fowl, cut into 4 breast and 4 leg portions

5–6 sprigs of thyme

8 slices pancetta or bacon

2–3 tablespoons olive oil

1 celeriac, about 500 g, cut into medium chunks

2 red onions, cut into quarters

8 small carrots, peeled and left whole

150 ml tawny port

500 ml chicken stock

750 ml full-bodied red wine, such as Rhône

3 fresh bay leaves

1 large cinnamon stick, broken into 3–4 pieces

1 tablespoon unsalted butter

1 tablespoon large green olives, rinsed and pitted

sea salt and freshly ground black pepper

SERVES 4

Lift the skin of each piece of guinea fowl, tuck up a few sprigs of the thyme, then season and wrap with the pancetta or bacon. Tie with kitchen string.

Heat the oil in a frying pan, add the bacon-wrapped guinea fowl (in batches if necessary) and sear until browned on all sides. Remove to an ovenproof dish. Add the vegetables to the pan, fry until lightly golden, then transfer to the dish.

Pour the port and stock into the frying pan and heat, stirring, to dissolve the pan juices. Add to the dish. Put the wine in the pan and heat until reduced by a third. Add the bay leaves, cinnamon and the remaining thyme and pour over the guinea fowl.

Cover and cook in a preheated oven at 180°C (350°F) Gas 4 for 30 minutes, then remove the breasts and vegetables and keep them warm. Baste the legs, cover, then return to the oven and cook for a further 35-45 minutes until cooked. Test with a skewer inserted into the thickest part of leg; the juices should run clear. Return the breasts and vegetables to the dish and return to the oven until golden.

Remove the guinea fowl and vegetables to a serving dish and strain the cooking liquid into a saucepan. Bring to the boil, then whisk in the butter – a little at a time – until the sauce is thick and glossy. Add the olives and heat through.

To serve, pour the sauce over the guinea fowl and vegetables and serve with mashed parsnips and buttered cabbage.

SLOW-COOKED PORK RIBS
with tamarind and star anise

Star anise is a sweet spice with an aniseed flavour – used in Chinese cooking. Here, it marinates into the pork to increase the meat's natural sweetness, while the tamarind adds a pleasing sour note to the dish. The apples help to thicken the sweet-and-sour sauce.

1.5 kg pork ribs in one piece, about 8 ribs

2 tablespoons seasoned flour

2 tablespoons unsalted butter

2 onions or 6 shallots, finely chopped

2 celery stalks, finely sliced

2 small apples, peeled, cored and coarsely chopped

150 ml Madeira wine

750 ml red wine, such as Beaujolais

1.25 litres pork or chicken stock

sea salt and freshly ground black pepper

MARINADE:

4 garlic cloves, crushed

2 teaspoons tamarind paste* or 1 tablespoon fresh lemon juice

5 star anise, broken into pieces

1 teaspoon black peppercorns, crushed

2 fresh bay leaves, torn

3 tablespoons red wine vinegar

a handful of fresh coriander leaves

4 tablespoons olive oil

Note: Tamarind paste is available from Asian markets or larger supermarkets.

TO SERVE:

chopped fresh coriander (optional)

Thai fragrant rice

SERVES 4

To make the marinade, put all the ingredients in a bowl and mix well. Rub it into the pork, then cover and let marinate in the fridge for several hours.

Take the pork out of the marinade and pat it dry with kitchen paper. Toss in the seasoned flour and shake off any excess. Reserve the marinade.

Melt half the butter in a heavy-based frying pan. Add the pork and sear until browned on all sides. Put in a deep casserole.

Heat the remaining butter in the same pan, add the onions or shallots, celery and apples and fry until golden. Transfer to the casserole. Stir the Madeira and half the wine into the frying pan and heat, stirring to dissolve all the sticky sediment. Add the rest of the wine, boil until slightly thickened, then pour into the casserole. Heat the reserved marinade and the stock and add to the casserole.

Cover and cook in a preheated oven at 150°C (300°F) Gas 2 for about 1 hour, then lower to 130°C (250°F) Gas 1 for a further 3–3½ hours, adding water or more stock, as necessary. Take care that it doesn't boil dry. When the pork is tender, remove from the oven, let cool and chill overnight.

The next day, remove and discard the fat which has risen to the surface, then reheat thoroughly. Add salt and pepper to taste.

To serve, slice the pork into ribs, spoon the sauce over the top and scatter with chopped coriander, if using. Serve with Thai fragrant rice.

Using a sharp knife or apple corer, make a cavity through the length of the pork. Stuff with the prunes and marjoram. Season with salt and pepper. Heat 2 tablespoons of the oil in a heavy-based or cast-iron frying pan, add the pork and sear until browned on all sides. Remove and set aside.

Heat the remaining oil in the pan, add the onion and garlic and fry until softened and translucent. Stir in the cabbage and apples, mix well, then add the sherry and vinegar. Bring to the boil, reduce the heat, add the sugar and stir until dissolved. Season and add the nutmeg and cinnamon sticks. Transfer to a large, deep casserole, top with the pork and add about 150 ml of the hot stock.

Cook, uncovered, in a preheated oven at 200°C (400°F) Gas 6 for 30 minutes, then reduce to 170°C (325°F) Gas 3, cover and cook for 1½ hours, adding more stock as necessary. Remove from the oven. The cabbage should be tender and moist and the pork meltingly tender with juices running clear. Remove and discard the cinnamon.

Slice the pork and put it on top of the red cabbage. Serve with mashed potatoes and fried apple rings.

Pork shoulder used to be quite fatty, so it was traditionally slow-cooked with fruits and sweet vegetables. Today, pork is much leaner but it is still delicious cooked this way. If you're not a fan of prunes, leave them out and stud the pork with garlic and marjoram instead. Season the cabbage well to bring out its full flavour.

BRAISED PORK
with prunes and red cabbage

2 kg boned and rolled shoulder of pork, rind and excess fat removed

14 no-soak prunes, pitted

3–4 sprigs of marjoram

4 tablespoons olive oil

1 large onion, finely chopped

1 garlic clove, finely chopped

1 small red cabbage, about 500 g, halved, central core removed and leaves finely sliced

3 dessert apples*, peeled, cored and cut into small cubes

2 tablespoons Amontillado or other medium dry sherry

2 tablespoons red wine vinegar

3 tablespoons brown sugar

¼ teaspoon freshly grated nutmeg

2 cinnamon sticks, broken into pieces

500 ml hot pork or chicken stock

sea salt and freshly ground black pepper

*Note: Use firm apples which hold their shape during cooking.

SERVES 4

125 g dried butter beans or
400 g canned butter beans

125 g dried cannellini beans or
400 g canned cannellini beans

125 g fresh or frozen broad beans

20 fat pink garlic cloves, 18 whole,
2 cut into slivers

150 ml milk

25 g unsalted butter

2 onions, finely chopped

2 celery stalks, finely sliced

1 tablespoon juniper berries,
crushed

1 sprig of thyme

500 ml pork or chicken stock

1.5 kg loin of pork, skinned

5-6 fresh sage leaves, torn

sea salt and freshly ground
black pepper

chopped flat leaf parsley, to serve

HONEY AND MUSTARD
GLAZE:

1 tablespoon mustard powder

1 tablespoon wholegrain mustard

5 tablespoons dry cider

2 tablespoons olive oil

2 teaspoons honey

SERVES 4

The aromatic, meaty juices from the pork soak into the beans, keeping them creamy and full of flavour. You can also use boned and rolled shoulder of pork, which is less expensive, but it will take an hour longer to cook.

HONEY and MUSTARD GLAZED PORK
with beans, garlic and juniper

If using dried beans, soak them overnight in cold water to cover, then drain and rinse. Rub off their skins with your fingertips (a simple but tedious job) and put the beans into a saucepan. Add cold water, bring to the boil, then simmer and cook for 5 minutes. Do not salt the water or the beans will become tough. If using canned beans, drain and rinse.

Blanch the broad beans in boiling water for about 1 minute, drain and put into a bowl of chilled water to retain their bright green colour. Slip the beans out of their grey skins and discard the skins.

Put the whole garlic cloves in a saucepan, add the milk and heat until just boiling. Remove from the heat and let stand to infuse.

Melt the butter in a large frying pan, add the onion, celery and juniper berries and fry until softened and translucent. Add the butter beans, cannellini, garlic milk and garlic, thyme and about 350 ml of the stock. Bring to the boil. Transfer to a casserole, cover and put in a preheated oven at 170°C (325°F) Gas 3 while you prepare the pork.

To make the glaze, mix all the ingredients together in a bowl. Using a sharp knife, make small incisions in the pork and insert the garlic slivers and sage leaves. Season with salt and pepper. Heat a frying pan until hot, add the pork and dry-fry until golden on all sides. Remove and brush with the honey and mustard glaze to coat. Add to the casserole.

Cover and cook for about 1¾ hours until the beans are tender and creamy and the meat is tender, but still juicy. Check during cooking and if it looks dry, add the remaining stock.

Remove the thyme, stir in the broad beans and add salt and pepper. Increase to 200°C (400°F) Gas 6. Return to the oven and cook uncovered for 20-25 minutes until the pork has browned and the beans are cooked.

To serve, spoon the beans into deep dishes, top with slices of the pork and sprinkle with lots of chopped parsley.

My grandmother used to make the best braised oxtail ever, so I thought I'd adapt her recipe to use sparerib chops. It's deliciously rich and sticky – and perfect with nutmeg mashed potatoes and braised root vegetables (see page 53).

BRAISED SPARERIBS in RED WINE
with cinnamon and orange

8 sparerib pork chops

2 tablespoons seasoned flour

4 tablespoons olive oil

1 red onion, chopped

2 celery stalks, chopped

2 carrots, cut into medium cubes

150 ml ruby port

750 ml full-bodied red wine

1.25 litres beef stock

3 cinnamon sticks

3 fresh bay leaves

1 teaspoon black peppercorns, crushed

5–6 sprigs of thyme

zest of 1 orange, removed in long strips

sea salt and freshly ground black pepper

SERVES 4

Toss the sparerib chops in the seasoned flour until coated, shaking off any excess flour.

Heat half the oil in a large, heavy-based frying pan, add the ribs and sear until browned on all sides. Transfer to a deep casserole.

Heat the remaining oil in the same pan, add the onion, celery and carrots and fry until golden, then add to the casserole.

Stir the port into the pan and heat, stirring to dissolve the sediment, then reduce until sticky. Add the wine and boil for 10 minutes to drive off the alcohol. Add the stock and remaining ingredients and bring back to the boil. Pour into the casserole.

Cover and cook in a preheated oven at 150°C (300°F) Gas 2 for 3½–4 hours, until the meat is very tender and falling from the bone.

Remove the chops to a clean container. Strain the cooking liquid in a sieve and remove and discard the cinnamon sticks, bay leaves, thyme and orange zest. Using the back of a wooden spoon, press the vegetables through the sieve and into the strained liquid. Mix well and pour over the chops. Let cool, then chill overnight.

The next day, skim off and discard the fat, then reheat thoroughly. Serve with mashed potatoes.

CASSEROLED LAMB SHANKS
with aubergine and tomato gratin

Serious comfort food. Braised lamb shanks can't be rushed, but you can cook them a day in advance. Then, once you've prepared the gratin, you will have a delicious meal in just over half an hour. I prefer them the next day because I can remove any excess fat from the dish before reheating.

Make small incisions all over the lamb with a knife. Stud with the garlic and half the basil leaves. Brush the shanks lightly with olive oil. Season.

Heat the oil in a large frying pan, add the onions, celery and carrots and sauté until lightly browned. Transfer to a large, deep casserole. Add the lamb to the hot pan and sear until browned on all sides. Put on top of the vegetables and tuck in the bay leaf and remaining basil.

Pour the wine into the pan, heat and stir to dissolve the sticky sediment. Add to the casserole. Heat the stock, then add to the casserole.

Cover and cook in a preheated oven at 180°C (350°F) Gas 4 for about 30 minutes, then reduce to 170°C (325°F) Gas 3 and cook for a further 1½ hours or until the meat is tender. Remove the shanks, let cool and chill overnight. Strain the cooking liquid and chill overnight. Discard the vegetables. The next day, remove the solidified fat from the liquid.

To make the aubergine and tomato gratin, heat 3 tablespoons of the oil in a frying pan, add the onions and fry until lightly golden. Remove and set aside. Fry the aubergines in the same way as the onions, then remove and drain.

Layer the onions, potatoes, and aubergines in a gratin dish, seasoning each layer and scattering with the olives. Top with the tomatoes. Season with salt and pepper and drizzle with the remaining oil.

Reheat the lamb cooking liquid until boiling and pour 150 ml over the gratin. Return the shanks to the casserole and add the remaining liquid. Cook both dishes in a preheated oven at 180°C (350°F) Gas 4 for 30-40 minutes until the vegetables are cooked and the lamb is heated through. Serve the lamb on top of the gratin and scatter with rosemary leaves.

4 lamb shanks

2 garlic cloves, cut into slivers

a handful of fresh basil leaves

2 tablespoons olive oil, for frying, plus extra for brushing

2 onions, skins on and thickly sliced

2 sticks celery, thickly sliced

2 organic carrots, unpeeled and thickly sliced

1 fresh bay leaf

250 ml light red wine such as pinot noir

500 ml lamb stock

sea salt and freshly ground black pepper

AUBERGINE AND TOMATO GRATIN:

5 tablespoons olive oil

2 red onions, finely sliced

3 thin aubergines, finely sliced and dried well

2 potatoes, par-boiled in salted water, then thinly sliced

2 tablespoons black olives in oil, drained and pitted

8 plum tomatoes, thickly sliced

150 ml lamb stock from the shanks (see method)

sea salt and freshly ground black pepper

rosemary sprigs, to serve

SERVES 4

Make small incisions all over the lamb with a sharp knife. Stud with the garlic and the leaves from one sprig of rosemary. Season the lamb.

Heat a cast-iron or heavy-based frying pan until hot, add the lamb and dry-fry on all sides to brown and seal in the juices. Remove and set aside.

Melt the butter in the hot pan, add the shallots and sweet potatoes and fry, shaking the pan from time to time, until the vegetables are lightly browned and coated in butter. Transfer to a large, shallow baking dish.

Put the wine in the pan, add the bay leaf and the remaining rosemary sprig and bring to the boil. Stir in half the hot stock, then add to the vegetables. Top with the lamb.

Cook, uncovered, in a preheated oven at 180°C (350°F) Gas 4 for 1½ hours until the lamb and vegetables are cooked, tender and browned. Baste 2-3 times during cooking to keep everything moist and add extra stock or water, if necessary. When cooked, the lamb will be pink in the middle, but if you prefer it well done, return it to the oven (without the vegetables) for a further 20 minutes.

Transfer the lamb and vegetables to a heated serving platter, cover and let the meat rest for about 5-10 minutes. Meanwhile, strain the cooking liquid into a jug, drop in a few ice cubes and let stand until the fat rises to the top and starts to set. Spoon off and discard the fat.

Put the liquid in a saucepan and boil until reduced and slightly thickened. Whisk in a few small cubes of butter, one at a time, until glossy and thick.

To serve, pour some of the sauce over the meat and vegetables and serve the rest separately.

1.5 kg boneless shoulder of lamb, trimmed, rolled and tied

2 garlic cloves, cut into slivers

2 sprigs of rosemary

25 g unsalted butter, plus extra for the sauce

24 pink shallots, peeled but left whole

3 medium sweet potatoes, cut into large cubes

250 ml dry white wine

1 fresh bay leaf

500 ml hot lamb stock

sea salt and freshly ground black pepper

SERVES 4

Pot-roasting is easy. The meat is browned with the vegetables to add extra flavour, then stock and wine are added. It is left to open-roast to concentrate the juices and at the end you have a ready-made sauce. Make sure you baste the lamb from time to time as it cooks to keep it beautifully moist and rich in flavour.

POT-ROASTED LAMB
with rosemary and sweet potatoes

Toss the beef in the seasoned flour until coated. Set aside. Heat half the oil in a flameproof casserole, add the shallots, garlic and bacon and fry until lightly browned. Remove and set aside. Add the mushrooms to the bacon fat in the casserole, fry, remove and set aside.

Heat the remaining oil in the casserole, add the meat and fry until browned (cook in batches, if necessary). Remove and set aside. Pour 100 ml of the wine into the casserole and heat, stirring to deglaze the pan juices and sticky sediment.

Return the fried meat and vegetables to the casserole. Add the bouquet garni, tangerine peel, stock and remaining wine. Bring to the boil.

Cover and cook in a preheated oven at 170°C (325°F) Gas 3 for 3-3½ hours until the meat is tender but juicy – the gelatinous parts will have melted to give a rich sauce.

To make the dumplings, sift the flour and baking powder into a bowl. Rub in the butter with your fingertips until it resembles breadcrumbs. Stir in the onion, thyme, salt and pepper. Add the milk and stir in enough water, 1 tablespoon at a time, to make a very soft dough.

Remove from the oven and increase to 180°C (350°F) Gas 4. Drop tablespoons of the dumpling mixture into the casserole. Cover and return to the oven for 15-20 minutes until the dumplings are light and fluffy.

Remove and discard the peel and bouquet garni. Serve from the casserole, sprinkled with lots of freshly chopped parsley.

1.5 kg shin of beef, cut into 4 cm cubes

2 tablespoons seasoned flour

4 tablespoons olive oil

30 shallots, peeled but left whole

1 fat garlic clove, crushed

100 g pancetta or bacon, chopped

250 g button mushrooms

750 ml full-bodied red wine

1 fresh bouquet garni (2 fresh bay leaves tied together with sprigs of thyme and parsley and a piece of celery)

dried peel of 1 tangerine

750 ml beef stock

sea salt and freshly ground black pepper

chopped fresh parsley, to serve

HERB DUMPLINGS:

100 g self-raising flour

½ teaspoon baking powder

25 g unsalted butter

½ small onion, finely chopped

1 tablespoon fresh thyme leaves

2 tablespoons milk

sea salt and freshly ground black pepper

SERVES 4

BRAISED TANGERINE BEEF with herb dumplings

Shin of beef is perfect for slow-cooking – it makes a rich, sticky, juicy gravy. It is also exceptional value for money. Let fresh tangerine peel dry out for a few days near a hot oven, then use it in the casserole; the citrus flavour of the beef sauce will intensify dramatically.

Rub 1 tablespoon of the oil over the beef and put in a large, deep dish. Break the ginger in half and crush one piece with a heavy knife to release the oils and flavour. Add to the beef. Peel the remaining ginger and slice into thin matchstick pieces. Set aside.

Cut the garlic head in half crossways, then put it beside the meat and tuck in the thyme and bay leaves. Add the beef stock, half the wine, peppercorns and 2 tablespoons of the oil. Cover and marinate in the refrigerator overnight, turning the meat from time to time.

Remove the meat from the marinade and pat dry with kitchen paper. Reserve the marinade. Heat a large, cast-iron or heavy-based frying pan until hot, add the beef and dry-fry until browned on all sides. Remove and spread the mustard evenly over the beef.

Heat the remaining oil in the pan, add the onions, carrots and celery and fry until slightly golden. Transfer to a large casserole. Add the reserved ginger matchsticks.

Strain the marinade into a saucepan and return the herbs and cut garlic to the casserole. Season. Heat the marinade until boiling.

Put the beef on top of the vegetables and pour over the hot marinade. Cover and cook in a preheated oven at 150°C (300°F) Gas 2 for about 4-4½ hours until tender, turning and basting the meat 2-3 times during cooking. Remove from the oven, season, then return to the oven uncovered. Increase to 200°C (400°F) Gas 6 and cook for 15 minutes until the outside of the meat is crisp. Remove the beef and keep it warm.

To make the sauce, add the remaining wine to the casserole and heat, stirring to dissolve the crusty sediment. Strain into a saucepan and, using the back of a wooden spoon, press the vegetables through the sieve and into the pan. Bring to the boil and whisk in the butter, if using, a little at a time, until the sauce is thick and glossy. Season to taste.

Slice the beef and serve with the sauce poured over, together with roasted vegetables and a sprinkling of chopped parsley.

4 tablespoons olive oil

2.5 kg boned and rolled brisket

7.5 cm fresh ginger

1 whole head pink garlic, unpeeled

7–8 sprigs of thyme

4 fresh bay leaves

250 ml beef stock

750 ml red wine, such as Rioja

1 tablespoon crushed peppercorns

2 tablespoons English mustard

2 red onions, coarsely chopped

2 organic carrots, unpeeled and coarsely chopped

2 celery stalks, coarsely chopped

25 g unsalted butter (optional)

sea salt and freshly ground black pepper

chopped fresh parsley, to serve

SERVES 4 as a main dish, then 4 the next day when cold

SLOW-COOKED BRISKET
marinated in red wine with ginger and garlic

Since there is less shrinkage in a larger piece of meat, it is worth cooking more than you need. When cold, the rest makes a wonderful sandwich filling or may be served with a salad.

Inspired by the flavours of the Caribbean, this dish is rib-stickingly delicious. Chillies come in all shapes, sizes and colours – and varying degrees of heat. Usually the smaller the chilli the hotter it is. The exception is the very hot Scotch bonnet or habanero. I've used a mild jalapeño here, but if you prefer a fiery sensation, use a hotter chilli.

RUM and CHILLI BEEF CASSEROLE
with oven-baked squash

Cut the steak into thick rounds and put in a deep, non-metal dish. To make the marinade, mix all the ingredients together, add to the beef and toss well to coat. Cover and marinate in the refrigerator overnight, turning the meat from time to time.

To make the oven-baked squash, heat the oil in a flameproof casserole, add the squash, nutmeg, salt and pepper and fry until lightly browned and coated in oil. Set aside.

Drain the beef and pat dry. Strain and reserve the marinade. Toss the meat in the seasoned flour until coated and shake off excess flour.

Heat half the oil in a cast-iron or heavy-based frying pan, add the meat (in batches) and fry until browned on all sides. Transfer to a casserole.

Add the remaining oil to the pan and fry the onions, garlic and chillies until softened and translucent. Season. Add to the casserole. Tuck in the bay leaves and oregano.

Put the reserved marinade and stock in the pan and bring to the boil, stirring to de-glaze the pan juices. Pour over the beef. Cover and cook in a preheated oven at 180°C (350°F) Gas 4 for 1 hour, then reduce to 150°C (300°F) Gas 2 and cook for 1½–2 hours. Add the squash to the oven and cook both dishes, uncovered, for 40 minutes or until the meat is tender and squash is cooked. Remove the bay leaves and oregano.

Scatter chives over the squash and serve with the meat and sauce. Add extra chillies, if using.

1.5 kg chuck steak, trimmed

1 tablespoon seasoned flour

4 tablespoons olive oil

2 large onions

4 garlic cloves

2 red jalapeño chillies, deseeded and finely sliced, plus extra for serving (optional)

2 fresh bay leaves

3 sprigs of oregano

500 ml beef stock

sea salt and freshly ground black pepper

MARINADE:

2 red jalapeño chillies, deseeded and sliced

finely grated zest and juice of 3 limes

250 ml dark rum

1 tablespoon dark soy sauce

2 tablespoons brown sugar

1 tablespoon crushed black peppercorns

4 fresh bay leaves, torn in half

2–3 sprigs of oregano

OVEN-BAKED SQUASH:

4 tablespoons olive oil

1 butternut squash, peeled, deseeded and cut into cubes

a pinch of freshly grated nutmeg

salt and freshly ground black pepper

scissor-snipped chives, to serve

SERVES 4

2 litres vegetable stock

500 g basmati rice, soaked in cold water overnight, drained and rinsed

125 g unsalted butter

1 onion, finely chopped

2 garlic cloves, crushed

1 small sprig of rosemary, chopped, plus extra to serve

125 g no-soak dried apricots, cut into large pieces

100 g shelled and peeled pistachio nuts

a large pinch of saffron threads

black seeds from 10 green cardamom pods, crushed

sea salt and freshly ground black pepper

TOMATO AND **MUSHROOM SAUCE:**

4 tablespoons olive oil

1/2 small onion, finely chopped

1 garlic clove, finely chopped

1 celery stalk, sliced

1/2 yellow pepper, deseeded and diced

6 plum tomatoes, skinned, deseeded and diced

6 button mushrooms, sliced

sea salt and freshly ground black pepper

SERVES 4

PERSIAN RICE

A Middle Eastern dish, traditionally cooked on top of the stove. The rice is left to cook undisturbed so that a golden crust forms at the bottom of the pan, which then becomes the top when turned out. It's the prized part that everyone wants. This dish cooks well in the oven because you're less tempted to have a look at it or stir the rice, which would ruin the whole effect. Serve with a chunky tomato and mushroom sauce for a delicious meat-free supper.

Heat the stock and 1 tablespoon salt in a large saucepan until boiling. Add the rice, cook for about 4 minutes, then drain. Melt half the butter in a 16 cm ovenproof saucepan, add the onion, garlic and rosemary and fry until the onion is softened but not browned.

Mix in the apricots, pistachios, saffron and cardamom. Add the part-cooked rice and fork it through the mixture. Dot the surface with the remaining butter.

Stretch a clean, damp tea towel over the top of the pan, cover with a lid and bring the ends of the cloth up over the lid. Let steam in a preheated oven at 130°C (250°F) Gas 1 for 45 minutes; do not remove the lid during cooking. Remove from the oven — the rice should be tender and moist.

To make the sauce, heat the oil in a frying pan, add the onion, garlic and celery and fry until softened. Add the remaining ingredients and cook for about 5-6 minutes, until soft but still chunky.

To unmould the rice, run a palette knife carefully around the pan and turn out on to a serving plate so the golden crust is on top. To serve, spoon the sauce around the rice and top with sprigs of rosemary.

VEGETABLES

Fresh oregano is used throughout the Mediterranean and gives this dish a warm, earthy flavour. If you can't get it, use flat leaf parsley or chives instead. Flowering herbs look so beautiful and taste great too, so when in season, serve the vegetables with a scattering of purple oregano petals. They're delicious.

VEGETABLE TIAN
with mozzarella and oregano

Roast the peppers under a hot grill or in a preheated oven at 200°C (400°F) Gas 6 for 10 minutes or until the skins are charred and blackened. Put them in a plastic bag, seal and let cool. Peel the peppers (the skin will come off easily), then cut them in half and scrape out the seeds. Cut the flesh into thick strips. Set aside.

Heat the oil in a frying pan, add the aubergine and fry briefly. Remove to a plate. In the same pan, fry the onions, courgettes and garlic until just golden. Remove to a plate.

Add the wine and heat gently, stirring to de-glaze the pan juices.

Put the prepared vegetables and plum tomatoes in a shallow, ovenproof dish. Scatter with the olives and pour over the heated wine. Drizzle with the balsamic vinegar and sprinkle with half the oregano. Season with salt and freshly ground black pepper.

Bake at 200°C (400°F) Gas 6 for 20 minutes. Remove from the oven, dot the top with the mozzarella and cook for a further 10–15 minutes or until the cheese has melted and the vegetables are well-roasted.

Sprinkle with the remaining oregano and serve with crusty country bread to mop up the lovely juices.

2 yellow peppers

6 tablespoons olive oil

1 long, thin aubergine, cut into thick slices

2 red onions, cut into quarters

2 courgettes, cut diagonally into chunks

12 pink garlic cloves

250 ml red wine

12 ripe plum tomatoes, cut in half lengthways

12 black olives, pitted

2 tablespoons balsamic vinegar

1 tablespoon chopped fresh oregano

2 buffalo mozzarella cheeses, about 150 g each, drained and thickly sliced

sea salt and freshly ground black pepper

SERVES 4

Add the potatoes to a saucepan of boiling salted water and cook for 5 minutes. Drain and let cool for a few minutes.

Put a layer of potatoes in a greased 1.5 litre gratin dish and top with a layer of chopped onions. Add a few sage leaves, salt and pepper. Repeat, finishing with a layer of potato.

Melt the butter in a frying pan, add the apples and turn to coat well. Arrange the apples on top of the potatoes, slightly overlapping each slice. Beat the cream and egg until mixed, then add the nutmeg, salt and pepper and pour over the apples.

Bake in a preheated oven at 190°C (375°F) Gas 5 for about 50 minutes to 1 hour until the potatoes are tender – test by piercing the centre with a skewer. Remove from the oven.

For a golden, nutty top, flash-cook the gratin under a hot grill or use a cook's blowtorch.

1.5 kg waxy potatoes, finely sliced

1 onion, finely chopped

leaves from 3–4 sprigs of sage

1 tablespoon unsalted butter

4 Granny Smith apples, peeled and thickly sliced

250 ml double cream

1 egg

a large pinch of freshly grated nutmeg

sea salt and freshly ground black pepper

SERVES 4 as a main dish or 6 as an accompaniment

POTATO, SAGE and APPLE GRATIN

Perfect for the busy cook, the vegetables can be layered ahead of time, then topped with the apples before baking. The gratin is delicious with any braised meat, especially pork, and particularly good with Cumberland sausages.

Peel and trim the vegetables, then cut into medium chunks, but leave the shallots whole.

Heat the butter in a large frying pan, add the vegetables and cook, stirring over a high heat until lightly browned. Season with salt and pepper.

Sprinkle with the sugar and cook until the vegetables are slightly caramelized. Tip into a casserole and add the chickpeas.

Add the stock, thyme and bay leaf to the frying pan and bring to the boil. Pour into the casserole, cover, and cook in a preheated oven at 150°C (300°F) Gas 2 for 1 hour. Increase to 200°C (400°F) Gas 6 and cook, uncovered, for about 15–20 minutes until the vegetables are tender and glazed and the cooking liquid has reduced slightly. Season to taste. Serve sprinkled with snipped chives.

1 celeriac, about 500 g

3 carrots

4 leeks

2 parsnips

12 shallots

50 g unsalted butter

2 teaspoons brown sugar

125 g dried chickpeas, soaked overnight, then cooked unsalted until tender, or 400 g canned chickpeas, rinsed and drained

500 ml vegetable stock

4–5 sprigs of thyme

1 fresh bay leaf, torn in half

sea salt and freshly ground black pepper

scissor-snipped chives, to serve

SERVES 4

Chickpeas add a nutty flavour and buttery texture. Sautéing the vegetables first will caramelize their natural sugars to give extra flavour. Serve with meat or crusty bread.

BRAISED ROOT VEGETABLES
with chickpeas and thyme

Put the beans in a large saucepan and cover with twice their volume of water. Bring to the boil, then simmer gently for 30 minutes or until the beans are tender. Drain and reserve about 500 ml of the cooking liquid.

To blanch the pork or bacon, put the meat in a saucepan and cover with cold water. Bring to the boil, then drain. Using a sharp knife, score fine cuts across the rind of the pork or bacon, then put the pieces into a casserole.

Melt the butter in a large frying pan, add the onions and fry until golden. Stir in the mustard, treacle and sugar. Add the reserved liquid and salt. Mix in the beans, passata or chopped tomatoes and oregano or marjoram and pour over the bacon or pork. Cover and cook in a preheated oven at 150°C (300°F) Gas 2 for about 3 hours until the meat is cooked and rind is crisp. Check during cooking and if the beans have absorbed too much liquid, add boiling water. Add the Worcestershire sauce and lemon juice, if using. Keep the casserole warm.

For the glazed carrots, heat a heavy-based roasting tin on top of the stove and, when hot, add the butter, oil and carrots. Turn the carrots until well coated. Add the honey and salt and mix well. Roast in a preheated oven at 220°C (425°F) Gas 7 for about 10 minutes, stirring halfway through cooking. Sprinkle with the sesame seeds and return to the oven for a further 5–6 minutes until the carrots are cooked, golden and crisp. Reheat the baked beans, if necessary, and serve with the glazed carrots.

500 g dried haricot beans, soaked overnight in cold water to cover, then drained

500 g piece salt pork or bacon, cut into 2 pieces

25 g unsalted butter

2 onions, finely chopped

2 teaspoons mustard powder

3 tablespoons black treacle

4 tablespoons soft brown sugar

250 ml passata or 400 g canned chopped plum tomatoes

3–4 sprigs of fresh oregano or marjoram

1 tablespoon Worcestershire sauce (optional)

1 tablespoon freshly squeezed lemon juice (optional)

sea salt and freshly ground black pepper

HONEY AND SESAME GLAZED CARROTS:

25 g unsalted butter

2 tablespoons olive oil

6 large carrots, cut into chunks

1 tablespoon honey

2 tablespoons sesame seeds

sea salt

SERVES 4

The distinctive flavour of this famous dish comes from the salt pork. My grandmother used to make it with pork hock and black treacle, although traditionally it was made with molasses. If you are vegetarian, leave out the meat and halve the cooking time – when cooked, add a tablespoon of soy sauce and a swirl of olive oil to make up for the lost flavour.

BOSTON BAKED BEANS
with honey and sesame glazed carrots

4 parsnips

1 butternut squash, deseeded

4 tablespoons olive oil

1 small onion, finely chopped

1 garlic clove, finely chopped

400 ml canned coconut milk

150 ml double cream

a pinch of sugar

50 g walnut halves

salt and freshly ground mixed peppercorns

fresh coriander leaves, to serve

CURRY SPICE MIX:

1¹/₂ tablespoons cumin seeds

1 tablespoon coriander seeds

1–2 teaspoons caraway seeds

black seeds from 4 green cardamom pods, crushed

2 pieces star anise

¹/₂ tablespoon fenugreek seeds

¹/₂ teaspoon freshly grated nutmeg

1 tablespoon mild curry powder

1 garlic clove, crushed

olive oil, for binding

SERVES 4

You won't need all of the curry spice mix for this dish and what you don't use can be put into a screw-top jar and refrigerated. It is wonderful added to sauces, marinades or rubbed onto fish or meat before cooking.

CURRIED PARSNIPS and SQUASH with walnuts

To make the curry mix, grind the spice seeds and star anise to a powder in a spice mill or coffee grinder. Put in a bowl and add the curry powder and garlic. Mix in enough olive oil to make a paste.

Cut the parsnips and squash into evenly-sized pieces. Heat half the oil in a frying pan, add the vegetables and toss quickly to coat. Season lightly, then transfer to an ovenproof dish.

In the same frying pan, heat the remaining oil and fry the onion and garlic until soft. Add 1 tablespoon of the curried paste and cook to release the aromas. Add the coconut milk and cream. Season lightly and add the sugar. Heat gently, then pour the sauce over the vegetables.

Cover with foil and cook in a preheated oven at 180°C (350°F) Gas 4 for about 45 minutes or until the vegetables are tender.

Remove from the oven and scatter with the walnuts. Return to the oven and cook, uncovered, for about 15–20 minutes, until the vegetables are golden and the sauce has caramelized slightly. Serve with coriander.

Put the butter and sugar into a saucepan and heat until foaming. Stir in the rice, coating the grains until they glisten. In another pan, boil the milk until frothing, then gradually add to the rice, stirring. Add the cream, lemon zest and salt.

Scrape the seeds from the vanilla pod into the rice mixture, then add the pod. Heat until almost boiling, then pour into a deep, ovenproof dish. Cover with baking parchment to prevent a brown skin forming on the pudding. Bake in a preheated oven at 140°C (275°F) Gas 1 for about 2–2½ hours until creamy and thick.

Remove from the oven and take out the lemon zest and vanilla pod.

Spoon the pudding into 4 large ramekins and let cool until lukewarm.

Cut the pineapple and bananas into evenly-sized chunks and thread onto the satay sticks. Sift icing sugar onto the skewered fruit and caramelize under a hot grill or with a cook's blowtorch.

Dust the puddings with a thick layer of icing sugar and caster sugar and caramelize as before. Let cool until set, then serve with the fruit skewers.

25 g unsalted butter

1 tablespoon caster sugar, plus extra for dusting

75 g risotto rice, such as arborio or carnaroli

500 ml milk

250 ml single cream

1 strip of lemon zest

a pinch of salt

1 vanilla pod, split in half lengthways

4 thick slices of fresh pineapple

2 bananas

icing sugar, for dusting

8 wooden satay sticks, soaked in water for 20 minutes

SERVES 4

The quintessential nursery pudding – and the definitive comfort food. It's very simple to make and when served like this – with a caramelized sugar top – it is sophisticated enough for even the smartest dinner party.

RICE PUDDING
with caramelized pineapple and banana

PUDDINGS

8 Conference pears, peeled and cored but left whole

375 ml red wine, such as merlot

750 ml ruby port

1 tablespoon juniper berries, about 20 berries, crushed

zest of 1 lemon, cut in a long strip

3 tablespoons caster sugar

3 pieces preserved stem ginger, finely diced

2 tablespoons syrup from the jar of preserved ginger

3 teaspoons arrowroot, blended with 2 tablespoons of port

TO SERVE:

250 ml crème fraîche

1 tablespoon syrup from the jar of preserved ginger

finely grated zest of ½ lemon

SERVES 8

Simple to make yet stunningly beautiful. Choose well-shaped pears – ripe but still very firm, so they hold their form during cooking. I like the pears hot or cold, served with lots of lemon crème fraîche or ginger or lemon ice cream.

PEARS in PORT
with juniper and ginger

Stand the pears upright in a deep, ovenproof dish. Put the wine, port, juniper berries, lemon zest and sugar in a saucepan and bring to the boil, stirring until the sugar dissolves. Pour the mixture over the pears to cover. Stir in the stem ginger and syrup.

Cover and bake in a preheated oven at 150°C (300°F) Gas 2 for 45 minutes to 1 hour or until the pears are very tender (depending on ripeness). Baste them 2-3 times during cooking.

Remove from the oven and, using a slotted spoon, transfer the pears to a deep bowl.

Pour the cooking liquid into a saucepan and stir in the blended arrowroot until mixed. Bring to the boil, stirring until the wine syrup is smooth and slightly thickened. Remove and discard the lemon zest, then pour the wine syrup over the pears. Serve immediately or chill overnight: the pears will turn a deep purple-red and the spiced wine flavour will intensify dramatically.

To serve, mix the crème fraîche, ginger syrup and lemon zest until blended. Add spoonfuls of the mixture to the pears and drizzle over the wine syrup.

Delicious with clotted cream or a dollop of crème fraîche. This simple pudding reminds me of Christmas with its spicy aromas and mulled-wine flavours. To save time, I prefer to use dried fruits which do not require soaking. Available from most supermarkets, they are labelled 'no-soak' or 'ready-to-eat'.

MULLED FRUIT COMPOTE
with cinnamon and cloves

500 g mixed dried fruits, such as figs, apricots, prunes and apple rings, rinsed and drained

2 teaspoons arrowroot

500 ml dry red wine, such as Rhône

150 ml Madeira wine

10 allspice berries, crushed

5 whole cloves

1 cinnamon stick

1 long strip of orange zest

1 long strip of lemon zest

freshly squeezed juice of 1 lemon, plus extra if necessary

3 tablespoons brown sugar

100 g fresh blueberries

TO SERVE:

orange zest, finely sliced

lemon zest, finely sliced

caster sugar, for tossing

SERVES 4–6

Put the dried fruits in a casserole. Mix the arrowroot with 2 tablespoons of the wine. Pour the remaining wine and Madeira into a large saucepan and add the spices, citrus zests, lemon juice and sugar. Heat until the sugar has dissolved and the mixture is boiling. Add a little of the spiced wine to the blended arrowroot, stir until smooth, then pour back into the pan. Heat, stirring, until slightly thickened.

Pour over the fruits, cover tightly with a lid or foil and bake in a preheated oven at 150°C (300°F) Gas 2 for about 2 hours until the fruits are plump and the liquid is syrupy.

Remove and discard the strips of zest and cinnamon stick. Add extra lemon juice, if the compote is too sweet. Add the blueberries, let cool, then chill. To serve, toss the finely sliced orange and lemon zest in sugar and sprinkle on top of the compote.

Slow-cooked until velvety smooth, this tangy pudding is heavenly. Cooking the cream in individual ramekins is also simple - and takes half the time of the large one. If you do it like this, caramelize and serve the cream in the ramekins.

LEMON CREAM with praline crisps

10 free-range medium eggs

425 g caster sugar

finely grated zest and juice of 8 unwaxed lemons

500 ml double cream

icing sugar, for dusting

PRALINE CRISPS:

4 tablespoons sugar

6 hazelnuts, roasted and skinned

a 7 cm plain biscuit cutter

SERVES 6

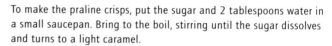

To make the praline crisps, put the sugar and 2 tablespoons water in a small saucepan. Bring to the boil, stirring until the sugar dissolves and turns to a light caramel.

Put the hazelnuts on a greased baking sheet and pour over the hot caramel. Let set. Break into pieces and grind to a powder in a food processor. Turn out onto a baking sheet lined with baking parchment and spread thinly to form a large rectangle.

Bake in a preheated oven at 180°C (350°F) Gas 4 for 2-3 minutes until melted. Remove from the oven and let cool for 2-3 minutes. Using a sharp knife, score triangles in the praline. Let set.

To make the lemon cream, beat the eggs and half the sugar in a large bowl. Add the lemon zest and juice and beat until mixed.

Put the cream and remaining sugar in a saucepan, bring to the boil and pour over the egg mixture, whisking as you pour. Chill overnight to let the flavours develop.

When ready to cook, strain the lemon cream through a fine sieve into a 30 x 19 x 3.5 cm baking dish. Put in a roasting tin filled halfway with water and bake in a preheated oven at 130°C (250°F) Gas 1 for about 1 hour or until just set but still slightly wobbly in the middle.

Remove from the oven and let cool until firm. Using a 7 cm plain cutter, press out 6 rounds. Carefully lift each one out of the baking dish and put on a plate. (Reserve the trimmings to serve another day with fruit.)

Sift a thick layer of icing sugar over the top of each lemon cream, then caramelize until crisp and golden with a cook's blowtorch or under a hot grill.

To serve, carefully lift off the praline triangles and lean them against the lemon cream.

INDEX